People-Watching, But Not Really

Cassandra Barcelon

BookLeaf Publishing

Presentation by *BookLeaf Publishing*

Web: www.bookleafpub.com

E-mail: info@bookleafpub.com

ISBN: 9789357615518

First edition 2022

This book is dedicated to you for taking the time out of your day to read this. There are so many books to choose from. Yet lo and behold, you ended up with this one, or someone else gave it to you. Thank you, you are appreciated.

ACKNOWLEDGEMENT

Many thanks to BookLeaf Publishing for the opportunity to share my work with others. Thank you friends and family for the encouraging words. A shoutout to those willing to talk to me and share their story; thank you for the teachings and great conversation.

PREFACE

I chose this title because when I think of people-watching, you usually don't interact with the individual you're observing. Instead, you watch, then move on to your next task for the day or whoever grabs your attention afterward. However, after a bit, I acknowledged the person and asked if they were willing to have a conversation.

Resign

Stimulate my mind.
Please don't waste my time.
I don't want to play our memories on rewind.
I want to reach another level, and you're falling behind.
Nothing left to do but resign.

Can't Be Compared

Anointed, intelligence never disappointed.
A voice so smooth, sure to unveil the truth.
Kissed by the sun can't be compared to anyone.

Bruised

I woke up bruised; not the first time I'd seen
these hues.
Struggling to remember anything.
Thoughts of happiness are fleeting.
I have lost myself trying to please you.
My leaving is long overdue.

Commotion

Left in the shadows with their wings clipped.
Their freedom was stripped.
It was excruciating.
No time for hesitating.
A plan was set in motion.
There was sure to be commotion.

Dancing With Leaves

5

Dancing with leaves.
Hair tousled by the breeze.
Beautiful creature.
Thriving in nature.

Your Eyes

Your eyes are reminiscent of sunshine.
It's otherworldly when they glimpse into mine.
Our souls are connected.
We are divinely protected.

All Alone

Bathed in the moonlight.
There was something about tonight.
An eerie feeling swept over the place.
No one dared to show their face.
Far from home.
All alone.

Battle

A battle fought for so long.
People are shouting to stay strong.
I can't give up yet.
There's nothing I want to regret.
I am doing this for me.
My soul will later be set free.

Guiding Light

Soul felt captured.
Essence was draining.
Being felt manufactured.
You came along, strength was returning.
Life was going to be alright.
You are a constant guiding light.

Magnificent

You're magnificent; it's like your heaven-sent.
I prayed for you under the moon, not knowing
you'd be here soon.
Unprepared, but you like that and you sit down
for a chat.
This conversation brings about inspiration.

Reminder To L.O.V.E Yourself

Live Authentically
Own Your Space
Voice your thoughts
Ethereal being

Not New To This

Numb to the pain.
You're not new to this game.
It's the same routine.
You try to intervene.
Trying to tell you it's game over.
Hoping you'll lose your composure.
They're about to find out what a devout can do.
Especially when one remains true.

This Is True

I didn't know what I was missing until you came
along.
You're all I think about when I hear my favorite
song.
It still feels brand new like the day I first met
you.
There are no doubts that this is true.

You Planted

You say you've never grown anything or haven't
been successful.
Let me tell you that beauty surrounds you
because you've been faithful.
You've provided good soil so that seeds could be
sown.
You are blessed, so let it be known.

Humor To Cope

Humor is used as a way to cope.
Better to laugh than to mope.
They say it's better to cry.
I agree that's not a lie.
However, to do so in front of strangers would be
insufferable.
Only those I trust am I vulnerable.

Goodnight

Goodnight, silence enters stage left.
From the window, there's the moon.
Leaves rustle outside.
Eyes still open wide.
When no one was looking, sleep exited stage
right.
Now it is morning and bright.

R.E.A.D.I.N.G

Random facts and trivia
Educational, entertaining or both,
Addicting
Dramatic pauses caused by cliffhangers
Inspiring characters
No sleep
Get-togethers to compare and contrast notes

I'm Just A Book

It's my turn; how have you been?
You said it happened; when?
Quit reverting the questions to me again.
This life is plain.
I want to hear from you.
What are you going through?
Whatever you undertook.
Don't fret; I won't say anything; I'm just a book.

I Knew That

You tapped into your potential.
The effort and time were essential.
The vision was clear.
You had no reason to fear.
You were called as a vessel.
I knew that you would be successful.

I'm Healing

Heart palpitations.
Replaying old conversations.
Sweat in my eyes.
Not a surprise.
Silently contemplating.
Trying to understand this feeling.
Everything is unraveling.
However, with that, I'm healing.

Thank You

Thank you for allowing me to pet your dog
when I asked.
Thank you for that random story you told me in
the grocery line.
Thank you for complimenting me on an outfit I
was unsure about.
Thank you for laughing at my cheesy joke.
Thank you for inspiring me to keep going.
Thank you for believing in me.
Thank you for being here.